Multi-Versed Lyrics

By Tiera Porter-House

Dedication

Dedicated to any and everyone who's ever felt alone or misunderstood. You're never alone.

Description of Book Cover: This book cover was created by me, Tiera Porter-House. Color scheme: Black and blue. Giving almost a matrix, sci-fi feel. The words on the front and back of the book cover are actually the titles of the poems inside of the book. The graphics, quotes, and visuals inside of the book were created by me as well.

Regal Rhythms Poetry LLC
P.O. Box 317746
Cincinnati, Ohio 45231

This book is a work of fiction. Names, characters, places, and incidents are products of the author's imagination, or are used fictitiously. Any resemblance to actual events or locales or persons, living or dead, is entirely coincidental.

Library of Congress Cataloging-in-Publication Data is available upon request.

All rights reserved. No part of this book may be reproduced in any form or by any means whatsoever. For information write Regal Rhythms Poetry LLC.

Cover design: Tiera Porter-House
Editor: Regal Rhythms Poetry LLC

Manufactured in the United States of America
ISBN: 979-8-9879871-0-0
Ebook ISBN: 979-8-9879871-1-7

Table of Contents

Made Alive 6

Nature Gang 7

Malfunctioned Temporarily 8

Rushing Weeds 9

Sugar-Coated Sh* 10

Happy Toxic 11

The Scatter 12

Earth Surfing 13

Spirit Talk 14

Hidden Treasure 15

Damaged 17

Higher Place 18

Healing Sensually 19

The Root 20

7th Sense 21

Gutter 2 Glory 22

Inner Knowing 24

Earth Speaks 26

Music My Eternity 27

Phoenix Rising 28

Glitch In My Memory 29

Encrypted Heart 31

Road To Sovereignty 32

"Illuminate the sky. Bring life. The cries help grow like rains from the sky. My light. I am. We are. We stars. I fell into myself like a baptism. I was cleansed from falsehoods and lies and introduced to love and light. I was freed from what almost cost me my sanity. I sank into love. It covered me like pool water. Drenched in high vibrations…" -Ti

Made Alive

Energy flows through me like chills... chills like a vocalist hitting the greatest note in a lifetime. Balancing out the faded wave of semi-sweet chocolate; intensifying its taste. Repeatedly swaying. Soaking in the environment's melody. Increased vision through spiritual eyesight. Seeing without looking; at other beings feeling the same majestic vibe. All souls rise and come alive. Who says dry bones can't live?...

Nature Gang

Crystals come together to fulfill their own purpose, no disturbance is required, and there's no need to be nervous. It takes courage to allow nature itself to work the miracle of nourishment. A covenant can't even save you if you have no focus. Dig deep into the dirt, let mama heal it where it hurts. First step is to have faith that holistic medicine really works. Funny thing is it's not modern medicine we're used to. It's the green tea, meditation, raw foods, crew. I wish to be there fully one day; I hope you do too.

Malfunctioned Temporarily

I'm not weak! Even at my lowest I'm growin' and goin' up on a ladder that I cannot see! I am strong! The battlefield could get real lonely, especially when the only one I'm battling is me. I ain't got no enemies. Open your blinded eyes and maybe you'll see. Even the physically blind have eyes that still see, and there's not a being in this world that can't mentally be free. I am not crazy. Temporarily malfunctioned maybe; trying not to get caught up in the excitement of the falsehood in "What's trending" …blending truths with lies. What a tasty apple pie. Forgetting about the dark witch who lured me in after she closed my eyes. Oh, I can see! With my best one in the center of my forehead that's connected to the heavens, and also continuously confirms the connection between you and me. This place that's connected to my heart space and intensifies my intuition that separates the real from the fake. Heavy is my heart and mind for those who do not see the great possibility of equality; that would rather scream at tall buildings, offending those who disagree. Refusing to realize that real change stems from personal change and accepting that responsibility. I am love. For true love involves no fear. True love is as real as the fact that truly we are here, together, in this room and in this space. Sharing each other's energies, feeding off of curiosities. We are not weak, but strong always spiritually. We are love, not crazy…just malfunctioned temporarily.

Rushing Weeds

I done played around too long. It's time to write another song about life and its unexpectancies and time's loyalties, because time is not a reality. It's a dream within a dream, forced to follow by society. Rushing…rushing through life then wondering where time went. Fenced up in the thoughts of other entities without following our own voice and thoughts. It suddenly becomes extremely vain and insane to scream, "land of the free!" We are still trying to obtain true freedom… of mind, of choice, of speech, and of voice; with no fear of being jailed for exposing the truth about darker forces. The light bulbs and of courses are popping out of the ground like pretty weeds. Awakenings are happening, regardless of who does or does not believe. Love seeds are finally sprouting, soon to spread their leaves, upward and outward like the life of a tree. Deeply rooted functions are rising from the ground and from the sea. A cleansing awaits from the hearts of you and me.

Sugar-Coated Sh*

Many lives have been claimed, for the sake of religious names. Force-feeding the fearful and slaying what remained. Love has nothing to do with this donut twist full of bullshit. I can smell the deceit and don't need eyes to see it doesn't fit. Pacifying lies and smiling with death on their lips, they're a trip!

Happy Toxic

It's the first sip, warm, and comforting to my chest. The hot liquid slides down, temporarily settling in my tummy. With every breath, it expands, and flows throughout my bloodstream. I sigh, with extreme satisfaction, and suddenly my whole body is warmed, from this chemical reaction. I'm relaxed, within the physical and mental. The fluid takes over, borrowing my body, like a rental. The cost is a good time, and a hangover tomorrow. Present-time says, there's no room for songs of sorrow. Happy is the best feeling, like floating on clouds. I smile, for the longest time, hot and happy for a while.

The Scatter

Another night again, spinning like the ceiling fan. Alone never, but it feels like it sometimes and I can't stand. I suppose, I might as well make good use of it. Prepare the future in the present time, hooking the line, for future good times. It's a good sign if you can read my mind. To me, that means your third eye ain't blind and it don't take a lot for you to realize. Realize the difference between a lesson and a prize. I am both. We are both. Hand in hand…electrified. I know it takes more than words to set shit right. Even if I am alone, I'm never alone in the light, nor in the middle of the night.

Earth Surfing

She travels in different time zones. She's different races. Many different faces. She traces her bloodline back to aliens. Astro American. No fighting, no fighting. Will love please get behind me, or in front for protection, cuz some other being is grimy. Can she float? Sure, but not on no gas, good dope. She has to find other ways to cope. Sing a note? Root beer float? Nope. The only way out is to go in. That's where her spaceship is…

Spirit Talk

I have a way of thinking beyond my thinking; going beyond my state of mind, growing up until old practices are declined. I am so convinced that I am more than I physically see, more than the blood that I bleed, more than my superficial needs. And, there is more we in me that molds my individuality. Maybe, I'm talking spirituality. I can label skin tones, and skinny verses "big bones; real breast and silicones until I'm called back home; yet and still none of that justifies the fact that I, the individual, still finds more than I, even more than three similarities in a totally different being than me. And this fact destroys the labeling fee. And this fact opens the doors to infinity. With all this thinking, or perhaps "over-thinking," I've allowed myself to go beyond my upbringing. No judgement at all.

Hidden Treasure

Not even comfortable in my own skin of well-blended sugar and spices, and diced tomatoes with cilantro. Deep inside, I know my value is of ancient gold, stolen, not sold, to an unconscious scheme of old. I could pay a thousand dollars to rise up and move out my space if it's distasteful.... Some would call it greatness, and some others might call it ungrateful. I can't save the one staring at me while I stare in the mirror. I am no one's inferior, nor am I the emperor, gazing down at the people who change like the temperature. I feel like a miniature. Compared to the vastness of space, in any given place. She's not how I pictured her. She's a manic, a beautiful darkness, an inner light being with her own personal signature. No wonder she feels so uncomfortable.

All troubled and bubbled up inside, her true power is in disguise behind fear. Peeking out when rage comes upon her; by then, she needs mantras and sage and incense too, to put her lower self, back in its cage. Then adrenaline rushes, over-exceeded functions, blood pumping like the engine that could, somebody please tell her somethin'. She has passion and doesn't know how to use it.

Damaged

Most damaged girls speak the same language without words, but through actions like choosing toxic lovers. Or no love, just sex. Strictly. Only covers. Or. Blocking out all sentimental emotions. Replacing them with anger. To feel too much is a danger. Feeling closer to strangers than family or close friends. Everybody is suspect. Rejected if you get too close, man. Hesitant on accepting a helping hand. Fear of alternative plans. "What you so nice for? I don't trust you." Another blocked door. Fear, sadness, regret, and pain burns like chemotherapy through the body. Praying for a cure for the traumatics. Trying to reach out to this or that and shit gets fuzzy-like…static. Love. Real love…Is the only thing that can cure the broken. Self-love grants us our first token.

Higher Place

Seeking higher places, these spaces on earth are too close. Veins overdosed on anxiety. I'm using that word way too much, like it's the life of me. Replacing my verbiage. Smooth as the curvage of my hips. Movin' over to bliss. Where I get sun-kissed and caressed by breezes and trees just wave as I pass by. And cries are joyful, not a sad tear in my eye, and lotus flowers bloom and tell of their survival out the mud. Yes, I'll trade fear for flourishing. Because the flavor is nourishing. Free of bound feelings. Limited, anything is sticky. So I seek higher places, cuz these spaces on earth are too close.

Healing Sensually

Touch. Me. Here. Not there, nearest my equator, nor deep in my core. But here in my heart, where feelings mean something, where love is everything, where I first met pain. Touch. Me. There. Caress the cracks, broken pieces from a painful past. Wet the hardest parts with your tears of compassion and mend those cracks back together like clay. Poke. At my brain. Find the missing link to what protects a scorned woman from pain. Expose my mental to a new way of thinking through your action. Undress me and touch. My. Soul.

The Root

The root, like I, grows… we are one. We can grow anywhere. Strong and mighty. Soak in the rain, and rejuvenate with the richness of the sun. One with the wind. We are. Taken for granted. The standards hold no value. I dig deep to discover my roots. The more I dug, stretched myself out, and I found another root. We grew together in numbers, in strength. We were oblivious as to what was going on above us. Great trees and plants of all sorts been growin' in numbers. Life was, is, evolving as we are. Underneath the ground, deep, and strong.

7th Sense

Separation is nonsense. My 7th sense says all is one, but then, there's the complex situation that chimes in when the two eyes see brutality across the nation. Is what we're seeing real? Is this how I want to feel? I don't, but what I see gives lower vibrational feels. Can I heal? While the world heals with me? Fake world tells me ain't no hope in trying, we have no hope, no need to figure out this "God forsaken" world. Eye see the same no matter who wants to blame. Love, real love, changes things. Like the paranoid thoughts of danger around the corner and everybody wants to hurt me. Love changes all things by moving forward and trusting. Love is in 7th sense and does not live in fear, but in presence. Knowing that presence changes presence.

Gutter 2 Glory

What if heaven had a ghetto? What if heaven was on Earth, and it was up to us to set the atmosphere? What if, we all held the same vision? What if it wasn't superstition to see things we don't understand? Too deep sometimes, diving into rabbit holes while some play in the sand.

To each his own, or hers.

Blurred vision,

Yet grounded in place.

Only seeing clearly, when I breathe slow, and deep.

And go back home,

Inside me.

Where I'm connected,

To Chi.

Where love is reflected. And I become We.

From the sand to the tree.

Where comparison is of no need.

We are One.

We all bleed.

Turn the pain into testimony.

Ghetto cries into symphonies.

Heaven on Earth,

From the gutter,

To glory.

Inner Knowing

Although I walk in the shadows of the night.

I will always remember that I hold light.

Illuminate the skies, do we.

Shine in the darkest times,

We do.

Breathe in the breath of life,

We do.

Connected to the breath that we breathe,

We are.

A mass of energy,

We are.

Souls having human experiences.

We are.

Waking up.

We are,

Remembering the Inner G.

I am,

Remembering the inner me.

Earth Speaks

Earth speaks like willow creeks,

Like soft footprints through dewed green lands.

Earth sings like birds at sunrises and sunsets,

Like breezes passing quiet ears.

She whispers to those willing to listen.

Earth heals like we heal,

Sheds tears that fall down mountains.

Feels pain within the same core that heals.

She breathes out love.

Whatever is not useful she takes and turns into fertilizer.

Nothing that was once alive,

ever really dies,

But is transformed.

The earth rises like the Phoenix,

Renewed, restored.

Earth breathes again like prana entering the body,

like a sigh of relief after long suffering.

Earth Speaks.

Music My Eternity

I could swim in music all day. Drink her elixir forever. Play under the cover with no rubber. Make babies for ages to come. I could dive deep in her waters to infinity. Climb her mountain to her highest peaks. Meditate by her creeks. She's the beep to my beep. I could sleep her, in dream state, and above into the ethers. I meditate her. She educates me. We lay up together by trees. She brings me to my knees. My melody. My perfect pitch and harmony. Music is my eternity.

Phoenix Rising

I take the ashes that fell from the hells that I rose from.

Illuminate the skies with the light.

That I came from.

Ashes went to fertilizer.

Nutrients for the food.

Grounded and still soaring up there with the moon.

Original afternoon at the highest peak.

Top of the day.

Full Sun rays.

A "no cloudy" day.

Instead of fighting fears, I invite them to stay,

And learn their origins and patterns,

Mold them,

This is my clay.

I put the fire to the vase.

No reason to run,

Nor to escape.

Flying up and out the way.

Fire burns to claim its place.

Glitch In My Memory

I walked deep into Euphoria.

Warm kisses like the heat in wintertime.

Breezes made love to my existence,

Crept into my lungs and filled her with the presence of life.

I kicked off my shoes and became one with the Earth.

She told me we had never departed.

I blew kisses to the sky,

My mirror image kissed me back.

So did the being standing beside me.

I closed my eyes for a while.

I saw nerves like branches,

And water, like my bloodstream.

Bones like the trunk of a tree.

Connection. Yes.

We had never departed.

Just a glitch in my memory.

But thankfully, without realizing,

I had walked back into Euphoria.

 I'll always come back to you.

Encrypted Heart

No constant intoxication from a mind awakened. Only a threat to those who like to control and call the poor forsaken. Only a tree has a bark that last for centuries on end. Roots deeper than rabbit holes, tellin' stories of the untold. And who cares enough to help provide for the rough. Be a guidance to the people who feel like life is not enough. Touch the hearts of those who think they are heartless, and that wealth is like gold. Fragile gangsta hearts. So sensitive, yet quick to kill. Until you walk in a victim's shoes, we all have stolen or steal somebody's happiness….or somebody's heart. What's a dollar to love, unmeasured value too far to measure love from the start. They got they own demons compared to mine; I can't compare. I can just be more aware my own consciousness in here. Raise my vibrations on a daily. Make an attempt to soak my mind on who society calls the blind. Stay focused on self-improvement. Be an illuminating light. Be the change I want to see. May we all be stars in dark skies.

Road To Sovereignty

I'm in a race, running, pacing for my Beverly Hills, but in the woods, in the country, all in nature at will. Where the freedom of breathing speaks volumes, with no noises. Musical birds singing, woodpeckers beating, making music, while the trees wave, dancing in the wind. Sittin' in my rocking chair with a pipe or cigar, Grandpa type. Daydreaming, while living my dream. Cool breezes flowing like streams. Clean water. Plenty, I mean plenty, abundantly. Worries are none. No need for the unnecessary. I work for what I'm hungry for. Living off of infinite wisdom, as my greatest store. A building up of infinite possibilities. Many riches, but not for greedy money thieves; retrieving from those so-called demon seeds. While kings and queens follow the Laws of Spirit and Earth. Not of man's so-called "good deeds."

PAUSE

Different realities start to merge, the urge to change comes in waves, glitches in the systems expose historical hidden missions.

www.ingramcontent.com/pod-product-compliance
Lightning Source LLC
Chambersburg PA
CBHW060622070426
42449CB00042B/2470